APPLE OF THE EYE

PARPUDI VENKATARAO

Contents

Preface

Children are the wealth of the nation. Metaphorically speaking children are the apples. But for the child society cannot exist. Children are the makers and constructors of the society. The child is also the maker of the adult. both the child and the adult are only the complementary and supplementary factors in an ideal family. it is only a cycle in which both the child and the adults take their places having their own relative importance. The child grows and develops in an ideal joint Indian family. The child enjoys all round development. A joint family is better than a nuclear family.

The purpose of this book is to focus on the psychology and progress of the child. He has not only his body but also a mind of his own. The child has his own tastes and talents. This aspect of individuality of the child grows along with the growth of the child.

In this context our respectful gratitude should go as homage to Dr. Montessori (1870) The champion of the rights of the child. Though a Roman she stood for the children of the whole world. She offers a strong hope for mankind to build the peace and progress of the children of the world. She evolved a system of education called Montessori system. A number of schools came into existence. The schools are named after her name.

The energy of the child properly developed is the greatest energy in the world.

Towards the end of this book, a number of new features like loose sallies, Quotable quotations, interesting thought-provoking proverbs are included to widen the interest and knowledge of the child.

Under the heading appendices many useful, Interesting and unique features have been included.

Simple and everyday English is used here. Even an average child is able to read and enjoy for himself.

A good book gives not only pleasure and knowledge but also wisdom. The good book teaches the child without a cane or a word of anger. The book never scolds the child but renders help. The book does not demand bread or money and available at any time. The author hopes and believes that this book will prove to be a boon to the children.

About The Author

The Life sketch of Sri P. Venkata Rao M.A. presented by Sriram Venkat Gonella the editor of this book.

Sri P. Venkata Rao M.A. was born in a small village near Amalapuram (Konaseema District) in an orthodox family in the year 1926. He is still hale and healthy at the age of 96.

Even now he wants to do some purposeful work. He used to tell us often, "*a wiseman will desire no more than he may get justly. He wants to use it soberly and distribute his money among his kith & kin and live contentedly.*"

The secrets of his sound health are contentment, sound sleep, moderate food and congenial work.

He was educated in the erstwhile PR College, Kakinada during the years 1942 – 1952 (both high school and college education) and loyal to his ALMAMATER.

PR College, in those days used to be the Centre of cultural activities and he was elected with thumping majority as the secretary (1950 - 1951) of the students' union. Next year (1951 -52) he was elected as the president of the same union. To be elected successively is normally difficult. It was a stormy political period. There was a struggle going on for united vishalandra. But he could not continue his political career.

Fortune smiled on him, he took the opportunity of working in the English department of SKBR college, Amalapuram. Slowly and steadily, he rose to the occasion of Heading the department of English and retired as Head of the English department in the year 1986, after a fruitful service of 3.5 decades with job satisfaction. He liked and loved his students in lakhs, and he used to call them all humorously, "*My academic children*".

His own grand children about a dozen are working as software engineers in U.S and U.K and other metropolitan cities, having settled in their lives.

Even as a lecturer never did he forget his hobby of service.

He associated himself with a number of service organizations like Rotary club and N.S.S.

He did yeoman service in the fields of children's education and adult education.

He was an active member of Rotary club Amalapuram between the years (1960 – 1970) and held the Presidential chair for two consecutive terms. It, indeed, was an honour.

For about two decades he was able to hold the post of being the Forum adviser of the SKBR College students' union.

He was a lifelong student engaging himself in his congenial work of reading and writing.

CHAPTER ONE

The Child Is the Father of the Man

This epigram seems to be strange. But this sentence simply expresses an idea with humour and basic truth.

The Very birth of the child is a divine miracle. The son and the father, the daughter and the mother, may differ now and then holding different opinions on certain aspects of life like marriages, dress, professions and other ways of life.

They are the representatives of different periods, values, tastes related to this everchanging world. Change is the unchanging law of nature.

The young and the old are no rivals. They are only complementary and supplementary factors helping each other in the evolution of mankind. what is more surprising in man is that his evolution never ends. But it is a truth. The evolution always continues.

The link that connects the past and the present is the child. He is the golden link between the father and the mother. The child is also a joining force of two families and two successive generations.

The child is the apple of the eye. He is the fruit of human evolution and the root of creation. This is the fundamental truth of life. Men and women are both creatures and also creators. However man is the product of circumstances over which he has no control. Finally, one has to surrender to the Divine will.

The Child, the would be social man is the constructor and maker of the adult. Both the father and the son are made up of the same stuff. They are bound to sail together in the journey of life. then only the life would be safe and sound.

There must be coordination and cooperation in the march of progress and evolution of mankind.

Old order changeth yielding place to new order God fulfills himself, in many ways, lest one good custom should corrupt the world.

So, this change is true and also necessary.

The epoch makers and harbingers are the children who are the representatives of this ever-changing world. They are the wealth of the nation.

The Intelligence of the child properly developed is the greatest energy in the world. God has given to the children certain special gifts. Growth and development through self activity. It is the greatest gift for the children. Children grow, learn of their own accord. They learn by doing. Still, they require the help of the adult and proper education.

CHAPTER TWO

FATHER AND THE SON

Father is the waning moon and the son is the rising star. The Fall and growth and decay are the natural phenomenon. They are only in the cyclic order and this order is the cosmic mandate.

The movement of this cosmic wheel, though appears to be slow and steady, is incredibly rapid and quick. What is true with the planets is also true with the human beings.

Father and the son are only cogs in the wheel of evolution and progress. What is most surprising in man is his evolution which is always upward having no end. This is the divine will and no one can escape from this.

However, man is subjected to many conditions of turbulence and turmoil. He has to swim against the current, facing many odds and ends. Man is able to withstand and move towards evolution which has no end.

Man, as an individual cannot do anything but in cooperation with some other forces, he is capable of doing something concrete.

Father and son though differ from each other, they are made up from the same blood and food. Father and son are only complementary and supplementary forces working in the evolution of mankind.

The sun and the Sire live under the same roof eating the same food, being brought up under same customs and traditions. Many hold different views of life. Because the son and the father are born in different times. They speak and act accordingly. The father and the son are the children of the times. They are not robots to be identical. But they are born with different tastes and talents. There are differences are there and they should be there. The difference is the sign of progress.

But for the differences society cannot flourish. Differences are the soil in which the society grows and develops. The differences between father and son, between mother daughter are common.

Their differences may lead to violent clashes of even bloodshed and permanent segregations on matters of marriage, matrimony and property. In the present bourgeois set up, the differences are there whether we like it or not. These are the bitter pills and we have to swallow.

The whole world is a cycle and place where every one can live very happily with mutual cooperation, provided both parties are free from mutual suspicions.

In the society and in the families, there are sons, fathers, mothers, daughters and grandparents. A family is a group of blood relatives with differences of tastes, talents and beliefs.

The family is not a group of toys well arranged, but a group of people with emotions, pride and prejudice. Of all, suspicions is the worst which creates dents to torment in the members of the family. The harmony in the family is disturbed.

Instead of becoming slaves to suspicions all the members of family should live together working hand in glove creating heaven on earth.

Father and son are no rivals. Inspite of their differences which are temporary in character. They are one from same stem. They should live together and walk towards the common goal of never-ending evolution of mankind. But for the son there is no progress.

If the rising son is the root of progress the ripe and mature father with an abundance of experience behind is the fruit.

CHAPTER THREE

MOTHER AND THE CHILD

But for the mother, society cannot exist. A mother creates the home preserves and conserves culture and inculcates moral and spiritual values in the children.

The mother is the integrating element in the family. The mother is an embodiment of patience, maternal affection cannot be bought and sold.

The modern psychologists say that children love independence and they say, "help us to do by ourselves. The spirit of independence is to be appreciated. The children have not only their bodies but also minds.

It is only the mother who can read the minds of their children. The child maybe a boy or a girl. The needs vary with the sex.

Generally, girls imitates the mother subconsciously. It is a point of commonsense daughters are the copies of the mother.

If the mother were to be a modern mother working in an office or a factory. Conditions and circumstances are different. The modern mothers have to face many modern ills. Modern solutions are to be found.

CHAPTER FOUR

GOLDEN LINK

The Link, that connects wife and husband, the link that connects two families, the link that connects two generations is the child.

Figuratively talking the child is a golden link in a chain of never-ending evolution of mankind

Children are endowed with certain mental powers which adults do not possess. Some of them are Divine Bliss, innocence, sensitiveness which are peculiar to children. They are all the prerogatives to children.

During the early periods of infancy, the child smiles at herself; even during sleep children smile now and then.

That is the first gift of God the child might be enjoying heavenly bliss at that time.

The child grows and develops himself. Now this is the best period for the child. During this period the child is able to identify the persons round about him and also the sights and sounds.

Knowledge flows into the child through his five gates namely his eyes, ears, nose, mouth and skin. The child receives knowledge and retains and stores in the mind. During this period the child has voracious appetite. This process of acquiring knowledge of the child is a special gift. This process of acquiring knowledge is natural and spontaneous. But an adult has to expend laborious effort for the acquisition of knowledge. There is a world of difference between child and the adult. As an example, a child masters his mother tongue with effortless ease. Spontaneous acquisition of knowledge is the characteristic of childhood.

Children have great enthusiasm and are ready for work with pleasure. Fatigue is foreign to them. Children are pure and innocent. They have not yet been polluted by modern ills and baneful culture.

Children are always happy and cheerful as long as their belly is full. Even the child in the arms of a street beggar maid is happy when her physical needs are satisfied. Their wants are limited and they are very near to mother nature.

Ninety percent children belonging to poor, lower middleclass families speak their mother tongue or home language. They can talk as they like; they can eat as they like. They are not worried about the next meal. They are alien to riches or poverty. These children are not forced to speak a foreign language. The poor children are perfectly free in every aspect.

Keeping aside the social aspect of the lives, it can be said that all children possess the natural gifts. The sum and substance are that the best period is their childhood. The most important trait about children is their adoptability.

The adult being less adoptable and the child being more adoptable to new conditions and circumstances society imposes on the child burdens necessary for the march of mankind.

Children are not robots; Children are not living machines but they are living flames having their own individual tastes and talents. Children have not only the physical hunger but also mental hunger and great enthusiasm.

As long as their sensitivity continues, they are always active and highly responsive and ready for action.

Carefreedom is their chief asset. In day-to-day dealings there is no harm to surrender to the wishes of the young.

"Old are the changerth yielding place to new.
God fulfils himself in many ways,
Lest on good custom corrupt the world."

CHAPTER FIVE

CHILD VERSUS ADULT

Children are sensitive. Childhood is a period of sensitivity and their sensorial organs are highly responsive. Their vital organs are active and their impressions jump into action. They are living flames consuming knowledge and absorb with effortless ease. Their five senses are five gates always open, receiving knowledge.

When Children are in their sensitive period, they full off activity and enthusiasm and remarkable activity. Rest and inactivity are foreign to them. They acquire knowledge automatically with out conscious effort. They are endowed with great mental powers with which they amass knowledge of various kinds.

Adults require laborious effort to act and learn. Children learn with pleasure and adults learn as a duty under some pressure.

Children are carefree and adults are in general, full of hurry and worry though rich and powerful. Children, though poor or gay and merry if their belly is full.

The intelligence of the child is the greatest energy in the world; Their intelligence is the source of development and evolution.

An average adult always suffers from either inferiority complex or superiority complex; both bring mental maundies. Both are equally dangerous.

Inferiority complex is the loss of inner strength of the mind. It makes man dull and inactive. A person suffering from inferiority complex is a dullard and a drawback in the society.

Superiority complex is more dangerous. He thinks highly of himself, he likes flattery he doesn't know that flattery is the food of fools. Fortunately, the child is free from these 2 things.

A foolish adult think that he can make and unmake his own child. His own child has both physical and mental hunger.

13

CHAPTER SIX

EDUCATION

Though the child learns by himself he requires some outward agency to prepare him to be a good citizen in the world.

Education is an aid and protection to life. Education should begin with the beginning of life itself. It is not confined to the four walls of the classroom. Children must be allowed to come into to the open world. Let them be in close contact with nature. Nature is the best teacher. It is not only to earn livelihood, but to lead a better life.

Scientific education is to be provided. Mere teaching of 3R's (reading, writing and arithmetic's) is not enough. ***"Teaching by the teacher and listening by the learner"*** is to be given up. let the children come out into the OpenWorld with an open mind. Let the children mix with one another. Then only the children will be able to get common sense. Common sense is uncommon.

Tastes and Talents differ from person to person. Children will have their own tastes. The teachers in the school the parents at home must bear in mind that the children shall have their own tastes.

The importance of the child and his education can never be ignored as he is the builder and the constructor of the adult man. The education of children is a lever with which great change in the society can be brought about.

15

CHAPTER SEVEN

LET NATURE BE YOUR TEACHER

Nature is an all-embracing term. All things animate and inanimate, come under the name nature. Everything has a purpose and a message to give. It is for us to accept and be benefited. Every message has a purpose and meaning.

The great apostle William Wordsworth (1770 – 1850) an English nature poet said and advised the people to understand and identify themselves with the spirit of nature. His message holds good for ever.

In order to give a spiritual and impressive colour to some basic truths of science, a method of dialectical dialogue is used to impress upon the children.

The following figurative talk, an additional attraction to children, is used.

Mother Nature Speaks: - I have got many children in my womb. Fruits, Flowers, Birds, beasts, suns, seas, rivers, forests, land animals, marine animals, insects, mountains and squirrels, big animals like elephants, wild animals, domestic animals, tigers and mild animals like cows, innocent lambs, fearful tigers and many more are there with me. As a mother I like and love them all.

Everything in nature, living and non-living has a definite purpose and duty to perform falling in line with universal plan. The little prig is as important as a giant. In the story "Squirrel and the mountain" the squirrel challenges and asks the mountain to crack a nut. The mountain asked the squirrel whether it could carry forests on its back. Each has its own limitations. This is the law of nature.

It is now the pleasant duty of the sun god who exhorts the people: -

"My Dear, you know I am a big ball of fire. You are indifferent or ignorant of my power. You do not know; I am a great boon to you. Countless benefits come out of me.

You must make use of me. you owe your existence to the life-giving radiation of the sun.

I am source of energy which is inexhaustible. This solar energy can be used for driving big machinery."

Energy: - energy enables us to work

A railway locomotive will never move out of station. There is some energy to drive the engines. They will not work for themselves. They require energy. God and Nature gives everything for men and women. The only thing is people must make use of all the gifts of nature.

CHAPTER EIGHT

LANGUAGE

Language is the dress of thought and reveals the personality of the speaker. It is also a vehicle of human thought and expression. Expression of a language is entirely due man's own effort.

Nature, the first teacher of mankind has given many gifts like light and air to mankind. The man has created and developed the language for himself. The credit goes entirely to the intelligence and prolonged experience of hundreds of living beings.

Climates and customs replete with different shades of religious beliefs and tastes. Hence thousands of languages have come into existence. Let thousands of flowers and cultures blossom and bloom.

A language having been born in many mouths and used developed by generations of people for centuries a language reaches a high degree of perfection as a vehicle of human thought and expression.

Now, the language is most powerful instrument of human progress ad evolution.

This is an endless evolution.

Language is born in mouths of children of 1 or 2 years of age spontaneously. The children begin to utter and produce some sounds like, "mom and dad" as their vocal chords begin to vibrate producing gentle sounds resulting in the birth of the babble tongue the language of the baby.

This babble tongue is the origin and birth of the sweet language, the wealth of the people. In course of time this language has resulted into rich language.

The experience and knowledge of one generation is transferred to the succeeding generations in the form of books containing the accumulated knowledge, of mankind related to the fields of science, art and philosophy.

This is a great linguistic victory and a feather in the cap of languages.

There is a mysterious urge in the child to go forward with the neighbors and their habits and customs with reference to their language and its use. The child is not a living machine but a living organism with a body, heart and soul with different tastes and talents of his own.

So the child contributes his mite in the birth, growth and development of a language, his mother tongue. The child has a wonderful capacity to master a language which is not possible to an adult. The child is endowed with a mental power which is different from the power of an adult.

A language is not a mere expression of ideas as it is filled with emotions, sentiment and personal feelings. A language is shaped and moulded the personality of the speaker.

A language has multiple purposes to perform. Even a child can express his feelings like anger, displeasure, joy and many more feelings. So, a language is a vehicle to express one's feelings, wants, desires, pain and pleasure.

Even a tender child can make use of this tool namely the language to build a base for his future.

CHAPTER NINE

ADAPTABILITY

The child is a living flame consuming and devouring all aspects of knowledge with his five senses, eyes, ears, nose, mouth and skin. The child is always alert and eager with his five senses to make everything his own. This is one of the chief characteristics of childhood.

There is a world of difference between the child and the adult. The child is more adaptable to new conditions and circumstances. The adult is always busy with his work and responsibility. The child is always fresh and eager to take up some activity. Activity is the basis. Activity, enthusiasm are the main properties of a child. To discharge his duties as a social man in future the child should be given some reasonable freedom; to develop himself in future the adult should not be a hindrance and obstruction to the child.

The most important duty of the adult is to help the child to help himself. The father or the adult should always be a friend, philosopher and a guide to his ward.

CHAPTER TEN

SCIENCE AND CIVILIZATION

<u>Science and Civilization</u>

Viewed metaphorically it can be said that science and civilization are the twin children of the mother nature.

Science means organized, systematic knowledge tested by experiment and found correct.

There is a yearning desire among the scientists to know more and more and unearth the latent facts and place them for further research. This process of research continuous forever having no end. So, science has been making magnificent strides. The scientists have come out from their ivory towers and begin to mix with the common people. The scientists shall place before the people the facts of his discovery.

Everything has two sides both blessed and baneful. As an example, the subject of atom may be cited.

The scientist has placed the atom and its energy before the men in power. The men at the helm of affairs shall naturally take the negative side of the atom and its energy to meet the ends of the existing times and the world has tasted the bitter side of the atom. The atom bomb was first used in the atomic bombing on Japan during the war (1939 – 45). The entire world witnessed the horrors of war.

Soldiers and sailors, airmen and civilians alike have suffered. Cities have been wrecked and aero planes were shot. Ships were sent to the bottom of the sea. This is the history of the hard realities.

Children are to be kept informed.

Children in general like to hear stories and play games at the same time they are to be introduced to the world of reality.

In dealing with the tender little angels. One must be very careful in dealing with the children.

During the 2nd world war, the then champions Mussolini, Tojo and Hitler wanted to provide education of regimentation and military efficiency. This is too much.

Instead of terrifying the children by showing them the dark side of science and the atom. It is better to show the better and utilitarian aspect of the atom.

It is the scientist, to be congratulated on his prolonged research work.

The scientists can show, this energy can be used for the peaceful purpose. In fact god has given the atom to be used but not to be misused.

CHAPTER ELEVEN

SOME SALIENT FEATURES IN THE EVOLUTION

1. The Child is the father of the Man, it is only a cycle in which both adults and children take their places having their relative importance.
2. Adaptation: The Adult being less adaptable and the child being more adaptable to new conditions and circumstances society imposes on the child burdens necessary for the onward march of mankind.
3. Having been used and developed by generations of people for centuries a language reaches a high degree of perfection as a vehicle of human thought and expression of the heart.
4. Books: Books are teachers without canes and words of anger. If we approach them, they are not a sleep. If we seek them, they do not hide. If we blunder books do not scold and they do not laugh at us, if we are ignorant.
5. Mother: The Mother creates and preserves the home. But for the mother society cannot exist. The mother

conserves culture and inculcates moral and spiritual values in the children and teaches them with patience. The mother is the source and the origin of all creation.

6. Work: work is worship. Work and rest must go together, mans work has changed the face of the earth. Purposeful work and congenial work give happiness to the worker.

7. Civilization: civilization demands more and more work; the marcher civilization is marked by man's increasing mastery of nature and his use of them for the service of mankind.

8. Accomplishment: accomplishment makes us happy. The happiness of having accomplished something by own effort is very great indeed

9. Never postpone till tomorrow what you can do today.

WORK IS WORSHIP

"Work is Worship", is not a mere Godly statement. Work with concentration is the first foremost thing for every man. Congenial work (suited to one's taste) makes a man happy and happiness is the good fortune for every man.

Work and rest must go together, work and rest must live side by side. Our hearts, blood stream will work and work till the end. They do not want any rest. Productive and purposeful work, unlike gambling and drinking, is of paramount importance.

We have no moral right to be idle. As long as we live, as long as we eat, we must do some work, the work one does should be useful to him or to the society. He who does not work neither shall he eat.

Man is the foremost worker in the creation. It is the human hand that has changed the face of the earth. If the man does not work nature remains as it is.

There are birds and beasts, animals big and small and many more living beings known and unknown, live and die for themselves.

But man being an intelligent animal live not only for himself but also from society in which he lives. But for the man there is no evolution of mankind. What is most surprising in man is that his evolution never ends. But always continuous. It is the human hand, human intelligence which are responsible for civilization.

Today man can run like a deer and jumps like a frog. By practice and training man is capable of doing wonderful things.

He can also exhibit histrionic talents in dancing and acting. The aesthetic histrionic element in the man is of the highest order.

The scientist has now come out he is able to talk with his kith and kin in foreign countries. He is also able to fly around the globe. He is also able to break the atom and do wonders

CHAPTER THIRTEEN

OLD AGE

Inspite of their age elderly people are important to themselves and to younger people also. Science makes old people live longer. Civilization finds less use for them

A Well thought rest house is enough for the elderly.

Old age is called the second childhood. Their wants are limited. Generally, men particularly elderly people feel that they did not avail the opportunities properly during their youth.

They must remember that the wheel of fortune never stops at a particular point. Omar says, *"Never care for dead yesterday or unborn tomorrow; take the cash in hand."* This statement holds good for ever.

A Wise old man says, *"The more one sees the world, the less he speaks; The more he seas the more he becomes wiser."*

Tolerance is a great virtue for men and women, Tolerance is an asset. A man of tolerance is liked by his own kith and kin. Tolerance is essential not only to the old but also to everyone.

Tolerance is needed in all walks of life.

Fights, quarrels, ruptures, frictions and in domestic circles.

Wars are common in all ages and in all countries. Wars are due to the lack of wisdom, foresight on the part of bigwigs.

The life of human society is too difficult to understand. None the less, states and civilizations rose and fell. Elegant houses built; factories are constructed; this is all forgotten history.

Unprecedented achievements came into existence in all stages of life.

A coin has 2 sides, so also human life has dual character. Everything is good in its time. This is the law of life.

Tolerance is marvelous lubricating oil which makes smooth running of the family.

Intolerance denotes lack of refinement and culture. Intolerance is the sign of narrow mindedness

A man, who is wise, is free from pride with prejudices.

A noble old man is one who bends himself according to circumstances. Generally, rich or poor; men or women; do not care for worldly things the only aim of old people is to spend their last days peacefully without creating problems to the youngsters.

The old have to cultivate tolerance and satisfaction it is not an easy thing they should not feel that they are ignored. They must bare in mind that a wise man can create heaven in hell. It is only the mind that can create heaven even in hell. But unfortunately, unwise people create hell in heaven.

Everyman has some importance of his own having accomplished something by his own effort, one feels and enjoys happiness.

CHAPTER FOURTEEN

APPENDICES

1. A Proverb is a wise saying of a great man. Which gives us refreshment to our minds and infuses new thoughts in us.
2. Old age makes us wiser and more foolish.
3. God will help those who help themselves.
4. God is truth and truth is god.
5. The mirror of god is nature.
6. God is the brain and man is the hand with which he works.
7. God's daughter is truth.
8. God's other children are beauty, sweetness, patience, prayer, forgiveness, and purposeful hard work.
9. Riches have wings.
10. Knowledge remains with us forever.
11. Kind words heal the wounded.
12. Purposeful activity is better than inactivity.
13. The evil that man does live after him.
14. The good that man does is buried after him.
15. We never know the worth of water till the well is dry.
16. The more you give the more you get.
17. One flower makes no garland.

18. Everything is good in its season.
19. A feather in hand is better than the bird in the air.
20. After a storm there comes a calm.
21. Dew drops do not quench thrust.
22. In a group say well or be still.
23. Words cut more than the swords.
24. Every man is the Architect of his own future.
25. Tastes and talents differ from man to man.

CHAPTER FIFTEEN

TITBITS

1. There is happiness in achievement and accomplishment.
2. What motivates activity is interest.
3. Happiness is activity.
4. Having accomplished something by his own efforts one feels and enjoys happiness.
5. Happiness is self-made.
6. Even tempered people are always happy, and their character is conducive to their happiness.
7. Mind is its own place; it can make a Heaven in Hell and Hell in Heaven.
8. Congenial and purposeful work is the secret of happiness.
9. The more you give the more you get.
10. Man is the foremost worker in creation.
11. Never Postpone till tomorrow what you can do today.
12. Teach and learn and learn and teach.
13. Say well or be still.
14. Live and let live.
15. Knowledge is power.

CHAPTER SIXTEEN

EPILOGUE

Man comes into the world naked and goes out of it naked. He is born free and later finds himself in chains, the chains being circumstances for which he is not responsible.

Some hold the view that he is a slave of circumstances; and some others hold the opinion that man is the architect of his own future. That is an age-old problem difficult to resolve. That is the crux of the issue which is too difficult to be understood.

Philosophers and men of religion differ from one another in their views regarding the above fact. with respect to this physical world of reality, matter, and movement.

Man being the most intelligent of all the animals can speak and write. He can also move from one place to another adopting himself to different climates.

What is most surprising in man is that his evolution never ends but always continues. In his everchanging evolution man can live making this earth comfortable.

From the earthworms to the marine animals, mountains, seas, rivers, plants and trees, birds and beasts, land animals all in nature help mankind. It is the man who receives help from all quarters.

Every animal and everything in nature has a special work to perform. Even the marine animals like the fish drink salt water many times their weight to keep down the proportion of salt water in the sea. Even the plants and trees consume poisonous gases to keep the atmosphere safe for men and life.

Some birds eat carrion and corpses in putrefaction. Thus, the purity of water and air is made safe for man.

Now it is for man to live happily keeping his head high. It is not impossible for him to live happily and making others to live happily following the edicts of religion and reason.

In the Famous Tagore's poem

Where the mind is without fear and the head is held high.

Where knowledge is free.

Where the world has not been broken up into fragments by narrow domestic walls.

Where words come out from the depth of truth:

Into that heaven of freedom my father let my country awake.